The Philosopher's Stone

The Philosopher's Stone

(A book about personal transformation)

By Raymond K. Hedgespeth

THE PHILOSOPHER'S STONE
Copyright 2015 Raymond K. Hedgespeth

ISBN-13:   978-0692527245 (Midnight Express Books)
ISBN-10: 0692527249

I don't wish to offend anyone; I make no excuses for my vernacular. I want to be clear so that there are no misunderstandings. I use the word "man" generically. It is meant to refer to the species of homo sapiens as a whole. It is in much the same vein as when women are referred to as 'guys' as in 'Are you guys going out tonight?' I make no excuses and no apologies.

Self-Published with help from

MIDNIGHT EXPRESS BOOKS
POBox 69
Berryville AR 72616
(870) 210-3772
MEBooks1@yahoo.com

The Philosopher's Stone

This book is dedicated to my friend Damien;

I hope that I help him find some of the answers to his questions.

"*I can never be what I ought to be, until you are what you ought to be.*" ML King

Foreword

All that man is or can ever hope to be depends upon his concept of God. We don't know what reality is. What do we know right now? What is it to be alive? What is this moment? What is living life this moment? Life is infinitely enigmatic. Life is a miracle. We've got to appreciate it. We are not living our lives, life is living through us. I am; I am aware. I have/am awareness. The I is our being, it is what we are. It is the subject of experience; the "I." It is the sense of being. Identify with "awareness." It is who we are. Consciousness.

God is a whole lot bigger and a whole lot more incomprehensive than anything that any theologian of any religion has ever proposed. God is a big mind that contains the cosmos and is becoming conscious of itself through all conscious beings in the cosmos. The mystery of God's search to know itself is echoed in us. The inner sense of God is a quality of deeper psyche and not of reason. We are the mystery of God dreaming it is human. We are the universal being appearing to be human. Get to know who you truly are. Know yourself.

Knowledge is central to Gnosticism, knowledge of who one really is.

Consciousness is what we are, when our ego dies, we are resurrected as consciousness of God. Consciousness is unchanging. Consciousness is our being, eidolon is our image. When we realize that our true identity is the Son of God; it is time for our eidolon to die. We will no longer identify with the eidolon and so will be literally selfless. The purpose of Gnostic initiation is to awaken in us recognition of our divine essence. We cannot die as we were never born.

When I was a boy; I heard about this stone, called the Philosopher's Stone that could turn base metals into gold. It was in a few of the tabloids, it was on TV, and I read about it in books; as I grew older and my knowledge increased as did my understanding. I also decided early in life to follow the man known to the world as Jesus Christ. I did have a little help from a fire and brimstone preacher though. Of course, it would be several years before I realized that they were connected in many ways.

This isn't a religious book; it is not a spiritual book, it is a book about personal transformation. I will refer to the Bible a lot because it is the religious text with which I most familiar and I find that it suits my needs. If there will ever be a revision and I find in other religious texts, or someone else brings to my attention references which will also accentuate the point, then they will be given as well in the future. Even if you are an atheist, or an agnostic, or if the Bible and its message are offensive to you, I ask that you take what you can and leave the rest. I promise you Atheist, Agnostic, Wiccan, Buddhist, Muslim, Tibetan, Hindu, and every other believer alike that there is a valid message here.

This conversion of which I speak is NOT about religion, it is about you and what you can do with your life.

THE PHILOSOPHER'S STONE

My father was Raymond Kenneth Hedgespeth; he was born on 8/26/45. He joined the Air Force when he was 17. I know very little about his youth. He was a very private man, and never really shared his life with me.

My mother is Patsy Laura (nee Scott); she was born on 6/5/44; she joined the Navy at 18. I know very little about her youth. She has been a very private woman, and never really shared her life with me.

I was born on September 30, 1965 on Offutt Air Force Base in Omaha, Nebraska. My name is Raymond Kenneth Hedgespeth Junior. When I was born, my mom was 2I and my dad 20. I was their first-born. My sister is Rebecca Kaye; she was born March 28, 1968 exactly 30 months after I was.

My mom's parents, Nora Juanita Scott (nee Strickland) (1923) and Leonard Winfield Scott (1912), lived in Dresden, Tennessee. My mom's brother lived in Skokie, Illinois. Lee; he was younger; I believe that my mother had an older brother who was stillborn.

My dad's parents lived in Campbellsville, Kentucky: Emma and Andy Raymond. My dad's sisters lived in Campbellsville. Kentucky. Caroline and Arlene; they were younger.

Sometime between Kaye's birth and Richard's birth, we moved to the Panama Canal Zone. We lived in Quarry Heights, Balboa, Panama. My brother is Richard Kevin: he was born January 23. 1970.

Just like so many other people who haven't given it a second thought; I ASSUMED that His first name was Jesus and His last name was Christ. Properly it is Jesus the Christ, even more properly it is Yahshua ben Yahseph the Messiah.

There is no letter J in the Hebrew alphabet, nor in the Greek alphabet or even in the Latin alphabet, the word/ name "Jesus" is Germanic in origin.

I was 8 years old when I first accepted this Jesus the Christ as my savior. My parents bought me a Bible; I no longer remember what translation it was;

2

though I am fairly sure that it was a King James Bible. I used to read my Bible every day. This was 1973. I had a 5-year-old sister and a 3-year-old brother. I remember it as if it were yesterday; it was when I first understood that this flesh ("I") was not going to live forever.

I prayed a prayer; I wanted to live to be a hundred years old; my sister and my brother and I would all die on the same day and we would all be buried in the same casket with me in the middle and them on each side of me.

As many people do; even card carrying Doctors; I believed that "I" am this sack of flesh. I believed that my life begins and ends with this flesh. I never thought about consequences. I never thought about what life is really all about. I only knew that I had to live a right life, my intentions must be noble and pure. If I am going to go to heaven, I had to get my life right.

For years, and it was all because of the Church, I believed that this flesh would be reanimated and when I would go to Heaven, I would do so similar to a ZOMBIE. Animated flesh, brought back to life,

3

the Resurrection, what are the chances that George Romero was thinking this same exact thought when he wrote, *"Return of the Living Dead?"* Seriously?

I understood that I was saved by my faith, and that by professing that faith, I was guaranteed a ticket to heaven; to spend the rest of eternity with Jesus and God. I understood that I show my faith by allowing the Holy Spirit that resides in me to dictate my actions. James speaks of works and faith. Faith without works is nothing. Years later, when I look back on my life, I am amazed at what I thought I knew and the level of ignorance that I was living in truly astounds me. Kids, though, right, what are you going to do?

As I read my Bible and I was able to comprehend it; there came some questions. What does Easter, the Resurrection of Jesus; have to do with Bunnies and Eggs? I didn't get it. If Jesus said that He was going to spend 3 days and nights in the Tomb, why does the Church teach 36 hours?

I begged and begged for answers that were based in logic. I understood even at the most basic level that being rational is simply insisting that opinions be

4

justified with valid reasons. I needed a valid reason to connect Peter Cottontail to Jesus. I could not swallow and would not accept that the Hebrew people would count a half a day as a whole day, who could accept this except those that want blind faith, something that I do not have.

My parents bought me a book for Easter one year; "*The True Story of Easter*" I remember it well, just not the author. The book was a large format; at least 12" X 12". It was about a ½ inch thick. Big beautiful color pictures, the artwork was beautiful. The author traced the history of the Easter egg to pagan fertility rites in Mesopotamia. I told my parents that I no longer wanted to participate in Easter as did other children my age. So, until I was about 13 years old, my mom and dad would buy models for me to build. I remember building a Superman model with him busting through a brick wall. I remember building an Incredible Hulk model with him bending backwards and his arms outstretched, fists clenched and howling to the sky. There was a Spider- Man model, I remember those well. I had others of course.

I realized even then, that I was going to have many questions; Adam and Eve, Cain and his wife, Noah and the Ark, and many, many more. I knew that I was going to be asking a great many questions. My questions were valid then and they are still valid today.

I could have never guessed that my questions would lead to challenging the Church, its doctrine and dogma. At ten years old, I would have never believed that listening to Andrew Lloyd Webber's *Jesus Christ Superstar* while on Church property would get me expelled from the Church.

But it did, years later, it was in the late 80's, but it did happen. I was listening to *Jesus Christ Superstar* on Church property, and the Pastor came up to me and asked me to leave and never return.

Jesus Christ Superstar is written from Judas Iscariot's point of view. Judas's question meant a lot to me. I needed to understand. His song resonated deep in my heart. The entire opera is asking a question about Him, who is He, man or God or both?

The Church taught me that God was omniscient. The very hairs on my head were numbered. He knew me in my mother's womb. He knew me before the foundation of the world. Because of this trait of Yahweh's I have spent my life plagued with a soul-scorching doubt. This doubt comes from my own desires to be in Heaven at the end of this stage of life.

I had Hell scared into me when I was a child. Every week for as long as I can remember the pastor would teach the same basic message; "Get saved or you are going to burn in Hell for all of eternity." I have often wondered, "Just how many ways are there to deliver the same message?" My desire to go to Heaven didn't develop because of a relationship with Jesus and meeting Him because He died for me. I was scared into my salvation.

My dad, Raymond senior, spent 21 years in the United States Air Force, when we left Panama we moved to Warner Robins, Georgia because he was stationed at Robins Air Force Base. My parents divorced soon after. My dad was stationed at the Pentagon so we moved to Alexandria, Virginia then to Bolling Air Force Base in Washington D.C. I found love in the arms of a man who decided that I should be a victim of his sexual proclivity and he would change me in ways that I have often wondered if there is a God in Heaven and He is real, was this all part of His plan.

As I grew older my quest for answers took me to all of the denominations. I have been to them all. I couldn't stomach the Hellfire and Brimstone sermons from the Southern Baptist Church anymore. I have been to every denomination of Christianity that there is, read their literature and found them all wanting for one reason or another.

It wasn't so much from hearing the same message week in and week out. It was that I understood (at least, on the surface, after all, I was only a kid) that there had to be more to going to Church than just getting scared into going to Heaven. After all, my Bible contained 66 books, each with a different message, but basically it all points to one general location; GOD.

So, when we got to Warner Robins, I looked for a new Church. I found one. Though I wasn't aware of it then, it was too late; the damage was already done. I had been forever scarred by the first Church that I went to.

Before I would leave this Church, I would begin to be plagued by questions that I have never been able to find answers to.

This Church, though I do not remember its name; it was a Baptist Church; but it wasn't the Hellfire and Brimstone Baptist Church that I was attending in Panama.

This pastor took a different approach; his message was based on the love of Yahweh and His Son, the Cross and the desire to see all men accept that Jesus died for us all.

It was an overwhelming love that Yahweh has for His creation. Because of this message being in such a contrast to the Hellfire and Brimstone messages that I had heard in Panama; I began to fully realize that there was a message in the Bible that was beyond the Hellfire's of Damnation.

This was a message of unconditional acceptance and undying love. It doesn't matter who you are,

9

what color your skin is, what bad acts you have done, it doesn't matter if you are rich or poor. It doesn't matter to God if you live in a cardboard box or a 120 room mansion. It doesn't matter to God at all, only that you have faith in His Son and that you believe that He died for you.

I would never be sure of any of my motivations for the rest of my life. I would always doubt my relationship to the creator of the human race. Is my salvation legitimate? No matter how much faith I have, is it enough?

I didn't come to my Savior and His Lamb on bended knee because I wanted to engage in a relationship with Him. I didn't come to the Savior and His Lamb because I was moved by His death. I didn't come to the Savior and His Lamb for any reason other than: "I don't want to spend eternity in Hell." I was scared in to accepting Him and His message. Oh yes, Yahshua/ Jesus is not the Savior, YHWH is.

Questioning my motives has been in the back of my mind around everything I do and have done for as long as I can remember, and not just the faith in

YHWH side of my life, but every portion of my life, EVERY motive is questioned.

"Can He see through this facade?" "I'm not going to make it, because He knows I am a fraud." "I don't deserve His sacrifice because I didn't come to Him in the right way."

"I will never be seen as worthy of His embrace." "I am a two-bit charlatan and He is just letting me fool myself." "Why did He choose me?" "If He created me why did He create me this way?" "If He is the author and finisher of my faith, why would He do this to me?" "What did I ever do to have this nagging feeling inside of me?" "Why did I have to have such faith?" "I know He is there, does He really know I am here?" "Where is He when I needed Him the most?" Get the idea? There are many more like it. I can fill up 20-30 pages easily and maybe more.

Don't get me wrong now; I know what the Bible says. I know all about the Blood of the Lamb covering my sins. I have read my Bible more than 300 times cover to cover. I have done in-depth studies on every subject from "Angels" to the

Resurrection.

I may not be like Jack Van Impe and be able to quote Book, Chapter and Verse of 10, 000 verses, but I do know the message of the Bible.

I know it well. I have poured over every single word. I have let the words breathe life into me. I have sought the face of YAHWEH more than once in my short and miserable life. I have been on bended knee. I have had my face buried in shame more than once.

I know what true repentance is.

There are four, and only four, (though I do imagine that there will be 5 before my life is over) pastors that have affected my life in drastic, more than thorough, at times quite rigorous, and in very demanding and exacting ways. These pastors are John MacArthur, Frederick K. Price, Pastor Paul Glass, and Pastor Melissa Scott.

I am more than reasonably sure that the 5th pastor would be Gene Scott, Melissa's late husband. I have only seen him on TV three times, I know that he can teach me, but I haven't yet been in a position where

I can purchase his sermons. I was flipping through the channels one night when I couldn't sleep and I saw Gene Scott on TV when he was teaching with a dry-erase board and showing me the scripture and the true meaning of the verse. The next hour was Pastor Melissa Scott. Over the next week, I fell in love with their teaching style. I had no idea at that time that he had already passed away. She is no longer on TV, (at least in this area).

I don't know if Petra could qualify as being a Pastor, I see them more as Evangelists, but Petra is responsible for changing my life in a couple of ways. They were definitely used by YHWH, in my life. It was during 1990, I will never forget walking down Main Street in Waupaca, Wisconsin listening to the "On Fire" CD, and dropping to my knees right there on the spot. I was hit right where I lived. I had let my guard down and I got smacked so hard that I was unable to continue walking.

A few years later, I went to live with the *Jesus People* in Chicago. I remember that the Pastor was the leader in *The Rez Band*. I think his name is Greg, but I am in more doubt of his name than surety of it. He would be another person who has been a tool in Yahweh's belt, in Yahweh's quest to break me. I was in service one day, and I felt the Holy Spirit hit me and I fell out on the spot. I was overcome.

I know what it means; to be "slain in the Spirit" it is beyond words. There is this overwhelming emotional response. It is not like vertigo. It is not like fainting. But, there is the washing over feeling. My whole body got really warm and tingly. It was like feeling flush or a hot flash. It feels so intense, it is nothing like taking a warm bath, and it's not like cuddling up with a blanket fresh out of the dryer. It is not like someone making a statement that relieves you of the intense pressure that you put on yourself to perform. It is all of this and more.

I have been on quest to seek His face. I wanted to be like King David, but with Elijah's blessing. Solomon asked for wisdom and was given so much more. So, I too prayed, I prayed for the wisdom to be His servant, to use me, and to guide me. I prayed the prayer but what motives did I have? Did I ask Him for Wisdom for the right reasons? Did I ask

Him for Wisdom knowing/believing that He would give me more?

The Lamb of YHWH told us, "He who would be first will be last, and he who is last shall be first. So, I asked to be the last.

I needed to find Him; I needed to meet Him on His terms. I have wondered almost my entire adult life if I am going to make it. I have sought the scriptures and read them over and over. I have listened to people like John, Fred, Melissa and Paul; for as long as I can remember. I have listened as the Hebrew, Greek, Aramaic, and Chaldean get torn up, dissected and put back together in ways that bring further comprehension to the Word.

I had it drilled into me, that for everyone who believes that there will be no favoritism by YHWH, we will ALL be able to perform the same miracles that Yahshua did, well for some reason in all of my belief, I can't even walk on water. There must be something that I am missing. I am equal to Yahshua in the eyes of YHWH because of my faith, then I want to be able to walk into hospitals and help cure the sick and infirm, there is no reason that a child should die of cancer. Yet for some reason I am unable to help. I must be doing something wrong.

The Dead Sea Scrolls, the Nag Hammadi Library, the Apocrypha and Pseudepigrapha from both the Old and New Testaments all have been utilized in my search to find His face. The Word is clear, "faith comes by hearing and by hearing the Word of YHWH." I have poured out my soul; I have emptied my being out. I have believed in the Word as it is written. The last chapter of Mark tells us that we can do the things that He did, and even more.

The publication of a Gnostic Codex brought to light a scholarly tradition to examine the scriptures with greater skepticism. *The Gospel of Thomas* and *The Apocalypse of Peter* imagines a close relationship with the Messiah.

I have seen the "*Q*" gospel. I have read the "*Gospel According to Thomas*". I have even read the "*Gospel According to Judas*".

I have wanted to serve Him by being a pair of healing hands. I have wanted to be able to bring His peace and love to the world. I have wanted to be "legitimate" unlike the frauds that get exposed. I wanted to be able to walk into hospitals, hospices, and nursing homes and be able to share His love and healing.

As much as I believe that He exists, as much as I believe that He is for real. As much as I believe that He was the Lamb on that fate-filled Wednesday afternoon, my hands have never been used by Him. Not in the way that I wanted to serve Him. This isn't to say that He hasn't used me, because I am convinced that He has used me in more ways than I ever could have imagined.

The doubt that I have suffered, has only been increased by this gap in my life. Instead of my faith dissipating; I searched harder and harder, "What is it that I am missing?" "Is it the way that I came to YHWH, is it because my heart isn't true." I need to know.

I learned relatively early on that it is in the process of studying that transformation takes place. I quickly understood that mature spirituality requires more than faith. I have realized that theologians know a great deal about God, but know little of

God. I say this not as an insult, I just understand that at least for most theologians it is doctrines that they focus on.

As I ventured deeper and deeper into religions, spirituality, mysticism, philosophy, and the like, I read many, many times that there is a considerable amount of allegory and symbolism in religious literature. For example, Mary Magdalene is often portrayed as having red hair. OK, Jewish people or Israelites have olive colored skin and black hair. Why would Mary Magdalene have red hair? I know there is something about the scarlet woman and red hair, I just have yet to find any real solid references to this so that I can understand what it all means.

It is this type of symbolism that is where we must look to find the truth behind the Philosopher's Stone. It is a symbol that has many, many meanings; but we need only concern ourselves with one of them.

The Philosopher's Stone is a symbol. It is referred to mostly in Alchemic literature; a literature that abounds with symbolism. I am not going to go into any of the symbolism of the Philosopher's Stone; I am not going to go into any of the literature that explores or examines the Philosopher's Stone. Again, this is a book about personal transformation.

Alchemy, the word, derives from Arabic. It was more than science. It was a fine web of linking actions with thoughts, magic, chemistry, philosophy and Hermeticism to sacred geometry. As an example I have given you the beginning of the Fibonacci Series - the successive Denominator is the sum of the previous fraction.

$$5/8 = 0.625$$
$$8/13 = 0.615$$
$$13/2I = 0.619$$
$$21/34 = 0.618$$
$$34/55 = 0.618$$
$$55/89 = 0.618$$
$$89/144 = 0.618; \text{ if you keep going,}$$
it will remain 0.618.

We know of the Alchemists because these were brave men who were hungry for knowledge; the Church's hatred for knowledge forced the Alchemists underground. The quest of the Philosopher is truth. Philosophy is a spiritual science. "Who am I" "Why am I here?" "What is my purpose in life?" The quest of the Philosopher is a long and arduous quest.

Dr. John Dee; he too was a seeker of this divine truth. Leonardo's drawings of the human being, he was a seeker of divine truths.

He who knows no life save the physical is merely ignorant; but he who declares the physical life to be all-important and elevates it to the position of supreme reality - such a one is ignorant of his own ignorance.

Only philosophy can teach a man to be born well, to live well, and to die well, and in perfect measure to be born again. The fool lives today, the philosopher lives forever. In my detail of the Stone, I am going to give a cursory exploration of how Gnosis and Philosophy are connected.

The Philosophical system that comes from India is known as Hindu as found in the 'Vedas' 'Upanishads,' & 'Katha Upanishad'.

The Alchemist sees things not as they should be but as they are. The mind sees & compares; contrasts, shapes and patterns. In the quest for turning base metal into gold, we must look at philosophy; it is a science and a discipline. One vein of philosophy is Gnosticism.

I saw more than once and never more than a passing glance that the Philosopher's Stone is an allegory itself. In my own personal quest for truth, never once did I come across a writer that ever went into any detail, but just to the tip alluding to it. I often began to wonder, did they really get it, or did they just glimpse the truth as through a haze, or a fog. They could make out the shape there in the distance, never drawing near. There, forever elusive.

I write to you, each and every one of you, I want you to be able to see that there is more to this Philosopher's Stone than mere fable or myth.

I have a friend, his name that I know him by is Damien Marcus Rudebush, though he was born with another name, Jean Raymond Presley; I have watched him struggle against himself for almost a decade now. This book is dedicated to him; and it is because of him that I write this. I have tried to teach him about the road that we walk. I have tried to teach him about dedication, discipline and perseverance. I have tried my best to teach that to

21

be the best in the world it takes much more than wanting something.

I found the Philosopher's Stone; in gaining this wisdom, I found it, I really found it. It is because I know that I found it; that I write this for more than my dear friend, it is also out of my love for humanity.

In many walks of life, man must be broken in order to find life. It seems to me, that the elders knew this and understood this ever since the birth pangs of man. The further back in time I travel, the more it is there. *(History and Archeology) My love for Star Wars* took me to the *"Journey of the Hero"*. My love for the study of the history of religion took me to Joseph Campbell, who of course is the foremost authority of the "Journey of the Hero" and the more that I studied the more that I learned, while I can tell you that I am on the verge of understanding, I can see the truth, I see it clearly, but it is as if there is a small point of clear light surrounded by a haze. I can see it; in the "Journey of the Hero" the hero must be **broken** in order to overcome his trials.

When America decided to become an industrial

nation, we lost something. That which we lost was and is something vital to our existence and our essence. I don't know that we will ever get it back, but I will try to help us reclaim some of it. Walking the road of inward growth is and must become once again fundamental to us as a NATION, as a people, as a race.

Today, in the 21st century of the Western / Roman / Christian / American domination of the world, the closest organization that we have to walking this much needed aspect of life, is the Free and Accepted Masons. There are other groups that teach the basic and rudimentary fundamentals of this essence. These are Alcoholics Anonymous, Narcotics Anonymous, and Sexual Addicts Anonymous and all of the other 12 step programs that have been born from A. A.

I am not a Mason; I would like to be a Mason.

According to Manly P. Hall, I am a Mason because of the intent of my heart to live a life that is worthy of the Creator. According to Manly, I do not need to belong to a lodge. My life is all I need.

The Philosopher's Stone

In "Lost Keys of Freemasonry"- I find the following statements:

"What is a Mason? He is a man who in his heart has been duly and truly prepared, has been found worthy and well qualified, has been admitted to the fraternity of builders, been invested with certain passwords and signs by which he may be enabled to work and receive wages as a Master Mason, and travel in foreign lands in search of that which was lost - The Word."

"Man's task now is to make flesh reflect the glory of that Word, which is within the soul of himself."

"The world is a school. We are here to learn, and our presence here proves our need of instruction."

"Every soul is engaged in a great work - the labor of personal liberation from the state of ignorance."

"Masonry is a structure built on experience."

"It is more than faith; it is a path of certainty. It is more than a belief it is fact. Masonry is a university, teaching the liberal arts and sciences of the soul to all who will attend to its words."

"Man is climbing an endless flight of steps, with his eyes fixed upon the goal at the top. Many cannot see the goal, and only one or two steps are visible before them."

"Hence a Mason is a builder of the temple of character."

"All who are attempting to attain mastery through constructive efforts are Masons at heart, regardless of religious sect or belief. **A Mason is not necessarily a member of a lodge.** In a broad sense, he is any person who daily tries to live the Masonic life, and to serve intelligently the need of the Great Architect."

However, I would still like to be recognized for my work by my peers, as it is our friends and family that help us walk a straight and narrow path and to keep from veering off and bringing disaster unto our lives.

I have seen it clearly as I studied the history of religion throughout the world, and was drawn into Freemasonry; I see the ritual of the Journey being played out. I see it so clearly. My book on religious history that is being written as I write this will go into great detail about it. We all must walk the Journey of the Hero to grow.

Getting back to the breaking. (See page 22)

As a person who has been trapped in the Criminal Justice system, I have became intimately familiar with a legal term known to those who work the field as "no known deterrent" in which most of America and other "civilized" nations are familiar with the idea that the death penalty does not keep people from killing one another.

As you read the following, I want you to bear in mind one thought. And this applies to everyone regardless of where you come from. I don't care if you are male or female. I don't care if you are young or old. I don't care if you are gay or straight. I don't care if you are fat or thin. I don't care whether you come from Beverly Hills, California, or from war torn Africa, the Middle East, China or Japan. I don't care if your God is: Jehovah, Allah, Zeus, or Ares. I don't care if you read and write in English, Spanish, French, Russian, Italian, or any other language on this earth. I don't care if you have a house full of servants, or if you are a servant. I don't care if you never read another book in your life, read this one; try to understand the message and then live it if you can.

The thought that I want you to retain is this; "In order for a man to change he must first be broken."

Breaking a human being is immensely harder than breaking a horse. The human spirit has an innate ability to bounce back from loss and despair. The vast majority of people can live through a tragedy and recover quite quickly.

There is a resiliency of this animal that is known as man; we can endure an awful lot. We can live through the devastation brought on by natural disasters. We can live on when a family member passes.

We can live through any number of tragedies. Our lives can be turned upside down by anything and we can bounce back from it without ever stopping to ponder it.

The ways that there are of breaking anyone is as

varied as there are people on this earth. I have been locked up since long before this latest conflict with the Taliban, Al Qaeda and the Middle East. Every so often as I was buzzing through the TV channels, or reading through magazines and newspapers I would read about the torture and the methods that we are using against our enemies to obtain information.

Torture and the counter to torture, that which most people overlook is that all the methods that have had to be devised are because of how truly resilient man is. We can take a considerable amount of pain. Our bodies and our minds can be conditioned to tolerate more than we know. Just think of a pugilist; the beating his head and his face takes. Ever been in a car accident? Ever had a severe toothache? The pain...

A woman giving birth to a child... the vaginal opening is mere centimeters compared to a baby's body. The pain that a woman experiences from giving birth is often immediately forgotten upon seeing the child. However, no matter how much pain she experiences and swears during that time that she will never do it again. She most likely will have another child; very few women have the uterus removed or their tubes tied after just one baby. The pain is in the past, forgotten. We are at once fragile and adaptable. We can overcome; our bodies are at once weak and strong. Our minds, able to forget can also never let go.

Every human being regardless of the source of the pain can adjust and even forget it. This is how truly resilient we are.

We are and always will be a work in progress.

This isn't just about physical pain; this is about all types of pain.

There is no other way; for a man to change he has to see the bottom of the well of despair and then decide to do something about it. There is a phrase, "I am sick and tired of being sick and tired," have you ever said it or heard it? The trick to changing is that no one can do it alone; we all need someone to walk with us. They are our support network.

Bear with me, there is a relevance to the Philosopher's Stone.

The prison system is the finest example; the revolving doors of the prison system spin both ways for many people time and again. Why? Because we (in this case, specifically prisoners, but it is true for everyone, generally) don't ever stop to think about how we got into this situation. For some, the adjustment to prison is not hard at all; for others though, it is a misery that is hard to describe. So many have the ability to just do their time, the time doesn't do them. It is the ability to adapt. I am on a unit with 4 guys who will play Canasta from breakfast, through lunch, past supper up until curfew every single day of the year. They never do anything but that. They are just doing their time without a care in the world as to how they got here. It is just this way with so many people every day all over the system. They do their time, not caring about today, tomorrow or even next week, month or year.

For me, the time is doing me. I need to leave. I know why I did what I did; I know that I can't do it again. I have spent hour upon hour, day upon day, week upon week, month upon month, year after year looking back at my life, and wanting something better for myself, I have been broken. I have been broken to the fullest extent that a man can be broken.

There is a torment that cuts through the deepest nadir of the soul. There is an anguish that is as black as the blackest night. There are caves on this earth, that without some kind of artificial light; there would be no way to see your hand in front of your face. This blackness; this despair; it is a weighty process being in prison for some people. Five minutes in prison can change a man forever. The hard part for most people outside looking in is that there is no real way to discover who those people are that can become damaged (severely damaged) by spending too much time in prison.

A man (or woman) can have his or her life taken from them upon entering a prison. You have lost your family, your job, your car, your home, your life's savings, everything. Everything that was taken for granted. During the period of incarceration, did you ever stop to think about how you got into this situation? Probably not. Why? This is because we are resilient and can tolerate just about anything.

Our adaptability is our own worst enemy. "We are our own worst enemy."

It is not just the loss of liberty that brings the pains; it is loss of control over your life. It is the loss of the ability to make something of yourself. The price that man pays when he goes to prison is a great one indeed. It is not enough to be branded, it is not enough to say that liberty is taken away; there are also freedoms that are taken away. There is a waste of life. The walls of the penitentiary do not just keep people from wandering out of prison; it also keeps the unwanted out.

If you don't have a life that allows you to be financially independent before going to prison; without some serious help; forget ever truly being able to make something out of your self

The Social Security System won't allow you to make deposits into the system. A 20-year-old man going to prison for 20 years is screwed out of living off Social Security in his 60's and 70's; it just isn't going to happen.

Getting a safe deposit box when you are on your

own on the inside to buy bonds for yourself and having a place to keep them for when you are released isn't going to happen either.

Of course, the biggest reason that the prison doors swing both ways for so many is that soon after being released from prison; the offender forgets the pain that he or she was suffering, this forgetfulness is part of our strengths yet it is also a great weakness.

There is only one way that an individual can change. There is no other way. There will never be any other way. There is nothing on this earth that any man or woman can do to change this. It is just the way that it is.

There is a greater truth here that we won't go into in any detail but it does need to be mentioned. There is the fact that every day of your life you change. The person that you are going to be tomorrow is different than the person you are today.

Every day that we live, we receive thousands upon thousands of bits of information; and it is this information which creates our identity, as our subconscious and consciousness makes use of this information it creates us; it makes us who we are.

So, we do change every single day; but there is a greater change that this work is about.

To convert an individual by outer means is useless, for true conversion can only come through the inner realization of certain facts. You can do immense and horrible things to a person, and it won't be guaranteed to have an effect. The experiences that we have, our perception of these events colors everything that we do. There is no such event as a bad experience just a wrong attitude. There needs to be some kind of recognition that there are many ways in which we train military and espionage personnel in ways to become immune to torture tactics. Much can be said about how these facts are portrayed in the movies.

How many people get violently ill when they have had too much to drink, and then swear to Almighty God in Heaven that they are never going to do it again, and they go right back to getting drunk the next weekend?

Getting out of the mess that you are in requires an understanding that; your situation won't change until you change the way you look at it. We live life having a variety of experiences and allowing those experiences to teach us how to live. New experiences place old ones in perspective.

The attitudes that we develop along the way; they are altogether different; they are on another train entirely.

I understood with crystal clarity that what wise people and grandmothers have always known is the way that you feel about yourself, your attitudes, beliefs, values, have a great deal to do with your health and well-being.

Memory is bound up with identity of the individual actor. Personal memory is selective; all is not remembered because it is not pertinent to the present. It is because of memory that we cannot escape the past. Even if the past doesn't exist, everything that has touched one of our senses is recorded.

There is a paradox here, you may not understand it

the first time through this book but if you will stop and think about all of this, taking all the time you need, you will grasp it, I promise you that.

I asked that this book be published in such a particular manner as to allow for many readings, and a margin for notes.

As you read through this, know this and understand it; the ways in which a man can be broken are as varied as he is. Everyone sees the bottom differently. A man must first be brought to the bottom of the well of despair. He must himself choose to change his life. He must first realize that he cannot continue to live the life that he has lived.

Everyone reaches this point in different ways. Many people are brought down through drugs and the devastation that drugs wreak on man. There are those who are brought down by alcohol, and there are those who are brought down by their weight, there are those who have ventured into crime, and have been to prison. The path is as varied as man, and just as the path is varied so is the bottom. No two crushing points of despair are the same. Man is a resilient creature; he can endure much. The stress and strains of life are nothing to most people. It is just as true that some men cannot tolerate the same things another can. Everyone's different.

No one can convince a man to change; he must come to this point on his own. This is the linchpin of life. Everything about our lives rests on this one point.

NO ONE CAN CONVINCE A MAN TO CHANGE; HE MUST COME TO THIS POINT ON HIS OWN.

Every person who has ever lived, and will ever live is a testimony to this blatant truth; no human being can be made to change; he or she must choose to do this on his or her own. The choice must come from within. It can be influenced by outside sources but that is all.

There is no easier way to say it.

How that choice comes to man; how do we bring it to him? That is the trick. There is no one logical thought, no premise for an ideal, no amount of persuasive talk, no torture, no discipline, no teaching someone empathy, no despair than can be inflicted. The choice must come from within.

The punishments that man can endure whether it is the situations that he brings to himself, directly or indirectly, whether it is the logic that he uses, whether it is the rationale that he applies to his decisions; all of this and more, man is capable of resisting change, by nature and by choice. All of this; has been a bane to corrections, the justice system and our societies for over 5,000 years.

The phrase, "There is no known deterrent." comes from Forensic Criminal Science. We have heard repeatedly that the Death Penalty does not deter anyone from committing murder. We know that the risk of accidents increases while operating a motor vehicle under the influence does not prevent drunken people from engaging in this irresponsible behavior. The threat of a lifetime in prison does not prevent people from repeatedly committing crimes.

There is just no way that we can create a system, a philosophy, a punishment, a plea, there is nothing that we can do or say that will prevent anyone from choosing to do harm to another.

There is no one way to break everyone. This is what is meant by the phrase; 'There is no known deterrent." If we could find a way to break everyone in the same manner; the need for the department of corrections would cease. The problems are many, and the solutions are numerous. The facts remain what they are; poverty, and social class, and our idea of individuality and responsibility and consequences are all a part of why we have crime, only God/Yahweh knows all of the reasons.

When it comes to change, there is only one way for this to happen.

There is only one way. Only ONE.

On his own, man must decide that it is time for a change. There is no other way. "I am sick and tired of being sick and tired," has got to be true, it can't be just said. It has to be felt. It has to be felt in the marrow of the bones. It has to be felt in the very atomic molecules of the DNA. There can be no doubt that the bottom of the well of suffering has been hit. If you only "think" that you have hit the bottom, then you haven't hit the bottom. The bottom must be hit, it must be hit hard. You can't hit it and bounce. You must lay there broken, battered, and bleeding. Severe hemorrhaging must occur. Imagine falling from a perfectly good airplane with a faulty parachute. When you hit, you don't bounce though. You hit, and you crumble. Bones break, muscles tear, ligaments detach, skin shreds, and you feel like you are going to die. While the EMT's rush to the scene, the minutes seem like hours, the hours seem like days. This is being broken. You can get up and do it again either wisely or foolishly.

That, my friends is why...

The Philosopher's Stone is the heart of a man.

There is no other stone. At the end of a man's life; if his life was not taken from him, and he is aware that he is leaving this mortal coil; he may look back on his ways. My dad was either fortunate enough, or it was his misfortune (depending on your viewpoint) to pass in his sleep.

My dad has been gone from this earth almost ten years now. As I write this; we are two weeks from the nine year mark. He was 56. He had a massive heart attack brought on by complications from type II diabetes. The passing of my father, and my dad (he is the same man) was but one element of my decision to become a better person.

Ever since he died, I have looked at life a lot differently.

Rhonda Byrne has exploded into the life of some modern Americans with her book "*The Secret*" claiming that the philosophy she is advocating and endorsing has been known for centuries is the way to a successful life. I did enjoy reading it. I am reading "*The Power*" now. She is missing one key point in her concept of successful living. It doesn't matter how much faith you have, it doesn't matter how positive you are, it doesn't matter if you shout from the rooftops of the world that it is yours for the taking and you can do this with 100% conviction; there must first be a breaking.

The heart of man must first break. Truly break. It must be a legitimate and soul scorching break. You have got to decide that your life must change; and how you get there is solely up to you.

I want to take you on a journey of awareness and discovery, there is a wealth of information that is there if we but know how to look.

There have been many books written on self-help and becoming a better person. I have read well close to 200 of them. Show me someone who has ever picked up a self-help book that has never been in some kind of dire straits. Show me someone that goes to an AA meeting that is not a drunkard. Show me someone who attends a NA meeting that has not been a drug user. People look for guidance when they are lost.

We cannot find the way on our own. We have to walk it, but we do not walk it alone; there will always be someone there. (Or at least there should be) if there isn't someone in your life, chances are not in your favor for success.

The walk cannot be done by another person for you. There are people who have made the journey that you will make, but you will be blazing your own trail. Just as no one will follow you or your trail, they may borrow from yours, just as you may borrow from someone else's. But, it will only be small sections. I cannot wear your shoes, I cannot wear your cap, nor can you wear mine. Each journey is an individual one. You may share with people what you have done; your friends, family, and peers will notice that you are not the same person when you finish this journey if you ever do finish it. Even as you walk it, they will notice changes in you.

You are a potter's clay in a shop. You are a diamond in the rough. You are a sculptor's slab of marble. The heart of man; it is a mess.

Our parents didn't raise us right, society as a whole is screwed up and we are trying to make the best out of what we have. By the time we reach adulthood in our society, life has been a horrible mess; we have been inundated with racism and prejudices of all kinds. The system has tried to crush our spirits and souls. We have even been devastated by the overwhelming numbers of people who are doing nothing but playing games with our hearts, souls, and bodies.

We lose our jobs, our homes, whatever. Some people take these things a little harder than others.

A man can turn to drinking or drugging as a way to dull the pain. There are so many people that live on the bottom echelon of society. They are the working poor. So many people in this country are destined to be the dregs of our society. It is said that the wealthiest people are a mere 10% of society; everyone else is middle-class and poor. There are over 300 million people in the US.

That means that 270 million people who will never be anything other than poor, middle class and upper middle class. All of them struggling. Struggling from one day to the next, never knowing what tomorrow will bring. This is where the bulk of our criminal element comes from. These are the people who are struggling to survive, the drug and alcohol users who drink and drug to avoid thinking about their pain. Some people are fortunate enough to avoid the morgue, but they may wind up in jail or prison. Some people are a walking time bomb.

The criminal; on average; is African-American, Hispanic or Latin-American, from the poorest corners of society. They are the rejected, the scorned, the ridiculed, the basest, and the contemptible. The lowest of the low, there are Caucasians in the Correctional system as well; they too are from the lowest classes of our society. The people who commit "White Collar" crimes; those of embezzlement and similar crimes are mostly Caucasian. They come from the upper classes. They are non-violent crimes. The criminal element of our society must always be; there must always be a class of people who do the "grunt" work, the laborious endeavors; the people who create the bridges, the roads, the houses, the service oriented like waitress, and clerks in stores. These people and those who exist on state created welfare, they must be.

There is a lot of pain in life.

When I began this prison sentence; I didn't know if I would live through the first year; those of you who know me through other works that I have written will know that I love movies; they are a passion and a past time for me. I saw many violent prison movies when I was growing up; and I knew prison to be a violent place. I truly thought that I might die within the first few weeks of prison; I wasn't going to be anyone's bitch. I would die before I suffer through being raped again. I made a vow that I would not leave prison the same person if I were lucky enough to survive.

The one thing that I have not been able to do is to forgive myself for destroying someone else's life. I read every book that I could find; from both religious and secular viewpoints. There were many books that teach why it is important; there are many books that tell you that if God loves you and forgives you that you should somehow be able to take comfort in that.

There are people who have written a vast number of books that tell you why you should forgive yourself, but I have never found one that tells you how to forgive yourself. It is through this journey of self-discovery that I have come to learn all about the Philosopher's Stone.

I may never be able to forgive myself for what I have done. Never. I read a book, whose title I no longer recall, once while I was trying to find ways that I could forgive myself; and the writer put forth the premise that if God can forgive me; who am I to question Him. It sounds like a truly legitimate question. Am I better than GOD, do I know more than Him, am I able to say to Him that I am better than He is at a judging my character? Who am I to tell someone that I don't deserve their forgiveness? I really did get a lot out of the book.

But, I still have to face what I have done. I can't repair the past, but for every second of life that I am given, I can do something to make the next one better for other people. I can live a right life.

I can have just and sound moral principles, and I can be a righteous person in the eyes of everyone. I can turn my life around and live to serve others.

I am not going to discuss my crime in this book; I am having another one published after this one that will discuss what I did and why I did it, and what I plan to do with the rest of the life that I have been given.

For now, let's just leave it at my discovery of the Philosopher's Stone has a lot to do with my desire to redeem myself

In so many ways, this is what the PHILOSOPHER'S STONE is all about.

Gold symbolizes immortality, as it does not corrode. Have you ever seen pure gold? I have.

Have you seen the sparkle and shine from pure gold that has been polished? I have. I know what is meant by the base metal into gold transformation. The shine is truly luminous.

I did some searching into the origins of some of our customs. Like the wedding ring. Most people have gold rings. I would assume the vast majority of people use gold rings. The circle, the gold, the vows; all work together. A Golden Circle, think about that. Gold is incorruptible. It can be broken, it can be melted, it can be shaped and it can formed; but it can never be tarnished, and it can never corrode. Gold is the purest of all metals. I am not a metallurgist and were I able to have access to either a metallurgist or more and better research materials I would be able to draw this out for you better. Gold, there is a reason that is it sought after.

Changing your heart, changing the base metal that it is, into gold; it is a process and it is one that is not easy.

You must see the errors of your ways, and want to do something about that.

For most people, prison life is a pattern, it is a pattern of day in and day out which becomes weeks. The weeks roll into months, and the months roll into years. As the years churn on by; a decade may pass, maybe two decades, and all that has been lost and missed hasn't begun to even dissuade or faze the average prisoner, it is not the least bit disconcerting to him. You can't miss what you never had. This has nothing to do with any mental disease, illness, or defect; it is how we are made as a species. Desiring a thing is not the same as missing it.

Look around you; see the despair and the tragedy all around you. See how we keep on living, see how we become desensitized to the world around us. We can walk by the homeless, and never shed a tear. We can see a neighbor's house on fire and turn a blind eye. We can see a crime happen and shut our eyes. The adaptability and resiliency of a human being is a marvelous thing indeed. Yet at the same time, it is the most terrible aspect of being a human. We stop caring.

Sometimes the victims of these tragedies will keep right on going about life. Never once stopping to think; "How did I get into this situation?" Some cry out to God, "I hate you!" "How could you let this happen to me?" More often than not, they will go on about their lives. The resiliency of the human heart is a remarkable thing indeed.

How immune we are. I was watching TV a few years back, and the cameraman and the journalist were talking about the state of litter that has been a problem, they were showing the rivers, creeks, brooks, beaches, and the many, many places where there were just loads of trash. I asked myself; why don't they clean up some of it? Why talk about it and just leave it?

As a nation, we have become desensitized to the world around us. In the major metropolitan areas, there are homeless people everywhere. At one point in the early 90's it was estimated that there were over 1 million homeless people in this country. I am sure that the number has doubled. We can drive along or walk along beside them without ever batting an eye; sometimes, though not very often, we turn our head in shame.

There is much about distrust in our world today. As

51

cities have gotten bigger and more and more people are coming into our country whether by birth, immigration or whatever, we have also become more complex, we no longer live in cultures where our neighbors are all on a first name/ friendly basis. Our neighbors today are frequently no more than a familiar stranger. We know their faces, we may know their name(s), but that is it.

We have grown distant and cold.

It is this hardened heart that must be changed. There is no other way.

The hardened heart, this is the base metal. How do you turn it into gold? Have you ever considered it? The refining fires of life are much the same as a real refinery. Gold; it is mined from the bowels of the earth. All that is mined, the earth and whatever happens to be in it, including the gold, is taken to a refinery. The metallurgist uses a refining fire to get the Golden Ore from the junk that is dug from the bowels of the earth. At the refinery, it is dumped into a vat; the vat is heated to over 1064° Fahrenheit. That which is not gold, the scum, rises to the top of the molten gold. It is sifted off repeatedly until all that is left in the vat is molten gold. All of the gunk must be removed from the human heart.

It is a refining fire. And so it is for the agonies of life, the suffering that we endure; the torments from those who would deride us; the distress from our jobs and the bills; the burdens of life in general; not to mention of the hardships that are added on because we burden ourselves with the problems of our friends and our loved ones. This is where the truth of the Philosopher's Stone lies. That which turns base metals to gold is life; more directly it is the trials and tribulations of life. We all have heard, "That which doesn't kill you makes you stronger." This is what life is about.

In the Bible, Jesus, or more correctly, Yahshua when talking to his followers mentions the road that we travel. He says that wide is the road that leads to destruction and narrow is the path that leads to life. There are two ways to look at this.

The first way to look at this is that the road is the way that we live our lives. The other way to look at this is that the road is people. These ways of looking at the path of destruction often overlap. The way in which we lead our lives is the road of life. This road is made up of the people who are in and around our lives who never give a second thought to who they are and what they are.

There are many, many people who are good people; they lead upright and morally just lives. However, there are people who are selfish, ignorant, caught in "me, me, me" of their lives. They don't think about the consequences of their actions.

The other road is nothing like that, it is the people. There are few people who are willing to walk a certain way of life. There are only a few people who are willing to do what it takes. There is a price to be paid. Are you willing to pay the price?

Life; it is not a path, it is not a faith, nor is it a religion. Faith includes sacrifice of reason. Faith is 'in' something, it has 'content' and "context." Faith on its own has never been enough, but it is knowledge not faith that has been forbidden. You need to have faith that deciding to do something about your life is going to have purpose and meaning; that it isn't for nothing. There is an episode on the FOX TV network show *House*, entitled *"One Day, One Room"*, Hugh Laurie and Katheryn Winnick are discussing that life must have some purpose; Adolf Hitler is brought into the equation; if monsters like Hitler have the same fate as everyone else, what purpose is theirs in life. This is where faith comes in. I recommend watching this particular episode.

Pick any vocation in life, it doesn't matter which one. There are always a select few who are willing to push themselves to be the best. There are guitarists who have pushed and pushed themselves to be able to become masters of the fretboard. There are pianists, who have become virtuosos. There are only a few truly expert marksmen. There are conductors that we call maestro. Mavens are a step above the rest of us, and there are always a select few who we claim have a rare talent in the field of acting. Not many people can lay claim to the title of genius.

Allegorically, I liken the road of faith to any one of a thousand occupations. There are always people who "settle," there are always those who won't put forth any effort. There are always going to be people who do a half-ass job. There will always be people who do "just enough to get by." There are people who will never put forth an ounce of effort to become successful at anything.

It is the same with living, there are always going to be people who don't think about who and what they are. They never stop to consider the origins of their thoughts.

There are people who never once stop to consider what a gift life is. There are people who never stop and think about what life is meant for. There are millions of people who never once have thought about the Earth that their children and descendents will call home while they rape and pillage and destroy the only home that we will ever have.

There are millions of people who have walked the face of this Earth content in living in the background just waiting to die; never making a splash, never reaching out to others, never once thinking that they have had a purpose for being here.

There is a pile of trash in the Atlantic; it is bigger than the state of Alaska. The currents of the ocean have created a type of vortex in the middle of the ocean where all of the trash that we have dumped into the Atlantic Ocean has gathered. People have done this, never once thinking about the impact that they will have on this Earth and their children.

To walk the narrow road is to suffer.

It is in the crucible of suffering that the greatest souls are seared and born; what are you willing to endure? How much are you willing to look at right in the fires of hell? Can you stand your ground because it is what you believe in? Will you tell others that they are wrong and you are right in the face of overwhelming odds? Where is your conviction? Stand strong.

I haven't read Nelson Mandela's entire book, "*The Long Walk to Freedom*" yet. I will finish it though. I have read a lot of biographies of people. Nelson's stay in prison, it was for 27 years. He was in prison for believing he was right. He committed no crime. Yet, he remained a positive man. I am sure that he had bad days, we all have them. He, however, is an inspiration.

Yet for this analogy, he is not a good example, there have been a few like him, people who never gave up in the face of overwhelming odds. We need a different role model. You can be sure that the people who put him there wanted to break him. And, they never succeeded. His heart remained true.

Raymond K. Hedgespeth

It is sometimes said, there are people who can't be broken. A perfect example of this philosophy is seen when, Michael Caine who portrayed *Alfred* in *Batman: Dark Knight* told Christian Bale who was *Bruce Wayne* that, "Some men can't be bought, bullied or negotiated with." While he was referring to Heath Ledger's portrayal of *The Joker*, the same thing can be said about The *Batman*. The *Batman* is not a man of compromise. We can learn a lot about ourselves and those around us from a variety of sources.

You have got to allow the people around you to affect you. When you are wrong, you are wrong; there are no ifs, ands, or buts about it. The only way to allow the potter to shape you and mold you; is to be affected by your surroundings. The local environment is made up of people and buildings, trees, flowers, and animals. The jeweler (life) must be allowed to take his time to bring out the best in the diamond. A diamond has many facets, and when it is prepared properly, the heart of a White Diamond is ablaze with fire.

When you are right, straight and true, and you are as

Nelson was, being wronged in the face of truth. Then please, by all means, do everything in your power to stay the course. The refining fires work just the same. The trials and tribulations that you are enduring, they are the potter's hands, the jeweler's tools, and the sculptor's chisel. The pain you are feeling is making you a better person, your character is being refined.

The greatest truth of our life is that we perceive things not as they are but as they're filtered through the screens of our own perceptual systems. *Obi-Wan Kenobi* (Sir Alec Guiness) in *"Return of the Jedi"*, told *Luke Skywalker* (Mark Hamill) that "many of the truths that we cling to come from our point of view." So many people in life do not have the time to care about this, they just go on living. We have jobs to do, houses to run, children to raise, spouses to care for. We don't have time to be bothered with the littlest of life's necessities. We allow people to tell us what to believe instead of going out to find it on our own.

A few years back, shortly before Dan Brown exploded into our consciousness; I was doing similar research to what he was doing with the *Da Vinci Code*. I read that Christopher Columbus is not who we think he is. The Spanish Inquisition took place in 1492. Care to guess when Christopher Columbus set sail? It was 1492. The Spanish Inquisition was carried out to rid Spain of undesirables such as the Jewish people. It is told to us that Columbus was given permission and funds by Ferdinand and Elizabeth to carry out his mission. This is a fine example of not believing everything we were told and taking it at face value. I will let you take these short simple statements and prove that there is something else here should you choose to explore it further.

In some ways this book too, is meant to provide you with information to lead you into an area of life that you might need some assistance in. Life must be lived. It must be experienced. We must become someone who is willing to push the boundaries of living. This isn't about becoming a maverick; or someone who is willing to risk everything in the way that some daredevils do.

As a person who has a strong attraction to

Hollywood; I have read a lot about directors, and producers who have pushed the envelope much as the ABC show from the Nineties *"NYPD BLUE"* pushed the boundaries of television censors.

Life; it is about discovering our own essential nature. It is about learning an inner knowledge which can never be truly understood from the outside. It is self-evident & beyond doubt. The real purpose of life is to awaken to our true essence. "Go where there is no path and carve a trail."

I grew up in the 70's and 80's; I was born in 1965. As a youngster in those days, there were a lot of Westerns on TV, I remember vividly Fess Parker playing *Daniel Boone*, and Clayton Moore playing *The Lone Ranger*. There was a TV show about Wyatt Earp. There was the *Rifleman* with Chuck Connors; *Have Gun Will Travel* with Richard Boone, Steve McQueen in *Wanted: Dead or Alive* and there were many, many others. These shows depicted men who were willing to push boundaries. They stood for what they believed in. Where are these men today?

Margaret Sanger went to jail for wanting to teach

women about birth control. There are others.

The message that I want to send to you is about this very strength, but it is coming from the *"other side of the coin"* in question.

We must be willing to change, we must be willing to look at our life and see that it isn't working the way that we want it to and find it within ourselves to do something about it.

Personal transformation is the process of becoming conscious of the bad habits that keep us asleep and replacing them with good habits that help us wake up. Personal transformation requires us to be honest with ourselves about our faults and foibles. The social system of which we are a part of works, and even exists, not only because of what we do, but above all, what we think.

The differences between the religions begin and end with some very basic tenants. Christianity requires a true devotee to repent of his or her ways of life. To see oneself as failing and falling short and to decide that there must be a better way.

Hindu and Buddhist philosophies are not for people

who are having some kind of crisis in life and looking for a better way, the religion of the Buddhists is the Philosophy of Sakyamuni. The Wiccan religion does not ask you to examine yourself either. The Koran and Islam are about service to Allah.

While each of these religions ask you to be the best person that you can be, there is nothing in any religion, with the exception to Christianity, that I have been able to find that truly asks you to look at your life and to see that you truly are nothing and that without Jesus / Yahshua and YHWH in your life, that it doesn't amount to anything.

In Christianity, life truly doesn't begin until you have seen the error of your ways and then decide to do something about it. There is a way to be a better person. There is a way to transcend suffering. There is no evidence we are free.

Had the Jews not been able to successfully make a case for their antiquity, the Christians would not have been able to acquire them as 'ancient' for their own. Even Judaism at its core is about repenting of your way of life. It is about service as much as it is about repentance. "Choose this day who you will serve." There is nothing in life without YHWH.

The process of awakening begins with (metanoia) which is often translated as *repentance* in the New Testament; metanoia is the signal that we are ready to embark on SOUL initiation. Repentance comes from the Greek - 'Metanoia' which actually means to change perspective.

Most people don't really understand what this word means. It means in plainer English, "to turn back." It is to realize that "I cannot go on living this way; I must find a new way of living. I need a new perspective of life." There is only repentance, there is no other. When we truly are sick and tired of being sick and tired and realize that something must be done. This remorse must be truly felt and experienced.

This 'metanoia' is the resurrection; this 'metanoia' is the awakening of the Christ or consciousness within the mystery as consciousness being what it is. This is where change truly begins; it is the only place that it can begin. There is no other way. No matter what anyone may think, believe, or opine;

change, lasting change, only comes once the heart cracks.

The one consciousness - being fully awake-fully aware-the Christ represents attaining this level of identification with the one.

The Book of Revelation in the Bible has in chapter 3 verse 18, and in the Book of Psalms chapter 12 verse 6: furnace, gold silver, "refining." Overall, the message of the Book of Revelation is an unveiling of the depths of the human soul. It is an allegory of the highest order. It is replete with symbolism. Every eschatological scholar knows this. Many people just disagree as how to interpret this symbolism.

However, the journey that I want you to take is this; the true (your) awakening is not of the body, but from the body.

Just as seeing the bottom of the barrel is different for everyone; so too, waking up is a relative or subjective experience, it too is different for everyone. The two concepts can even be considered the same. Waking up and deciding that you want to do something different with your life, the same message but different words. It is the context that matters more than the words that you choose to use.

There is a faith that is more than 2000 years old. This faith; was here long before Christianity was here. Long before. Most of the Church turned away from it; because they could not understand it. Even the brightest minds can sometimes be blind to things. I know mine is, I just don't get algebra at all.

There is a problem in this world that people give up things because they can't grasp the language, the philosophy, or the logic. There may be a struggle here, but don't give up. Don't give up. Learn to find that strength that lies within. There are two kinds of people in this world: those that are proactive in their life; and those who are spectators watching life pass them by.

(By the way, I want to gather together into one source all of the sayings; "There are two people in life, those that and those that." Send me all of the ones that you know and tell your friends to send me theirs as well.)

In the days of the beginning of the takeover of the world by Roman thought. There was a little bitty religion that was gearing up in the Middle East. We call it Christianity. Christianity didn't begin as one sect, which would become the Roman Catholic Church; there were probably as many sects of Christianity then as there are today.

With the discovery of the Nag Hammadi Library and the Dead Sea Scrolls, much light has been shed on the Middle East of the First Century CE. The old lies have had to be put aside, we truly now know that Christianity is not what we have been told that it was.

Scholars have always known that they didn't have the full picture, but in 1945 the scholarly world was ripped to shreds. Everything that we thought we knew has had to be rewritten. Even so, some of us still cling to those tenets that go back to the early years of Christianity. There are those who cling to these tenets as if they are the last thread and our very life depends on them.

There was one vein of thought that today we call Gnosticism from the Greek word meaning knowledge. Truly for all its worth, Christianity is not a new thing, it is older than anything Greek myth and Philosophy can offer; it is older than Rome itself. It is even older than Jerusalem or Baghdad, which is because of its Pagan elements. The fact is that the ideas behind Gnosticism, the Kabbalah, Ceremonial Magick, Yoga, and Philosophy all are far older than Christianity ever could be.

For countless millennia, men have been trying to discover that which makes us tick. Our motivations, our perceptions, and why we become what we do, and what it takes to truly become all that you can be. Is there a God in each of us, is it true that we are not humans having a divine experience, but a divine being have a human experience?

For this, Gnosticism is an ancient religion that demands attention.

There were ancient Gnostics that were a strain of Christianity. There is evidence that Gnostic Philosophy may have given birth to Christianity. I find it interesting that Christians would have the audacity to quote from their scriptures or condemn other faiths with such things as "beware of false prophets", or "thou shalt have no other Gods" in light of their own pagan origins. It appears, therefore, that Christianity could never be a pure religion, not when it is based solely on plagiarized Hellenistic/pagan beliefs twisted to be a means of controlling the masses.

Gnosticism is greatly misunderstood. I don't want to explain that misunderstanding to you in this work except to say; I believe that it needs to be looked at.

Earlier, when I was talking about knowing YHWH; and coming to Him, Gnosticism can provide some answers. Mainstream Christian Pastors are against Gnosticism; their message of Salvation by Faith doesn't mesh with Salvation by Knowledge. They misunderstand this application of knowledge. Or, they twist what they do know to keep you away from the Gnostics.

Simply put, and I do mean the simplest way, Gnosticism is looking at yourself at discovering what you truly are made of.

Can you tell me the origin of your thoughts? Can

you tell me why you have the ability to reason? Can you tell me why some have a stronger will than others? Can you tell me that you are not a divine being having a human experience? Can you tell me what it is to have an opposing opinion and why you have it? Can you look inside of yourself and tell me truly who you are and where you come from? Can you tell me why some men and women will run into a fire when everyone else is running away?

Gnosticism is not a bane to Christianity. It is a way. Not necessarily the way. It is one way of many to describe the Philosopher's Stone. Gnosticism is a mixture of Theology and Philosophy. The goal of Gnosticism is salvation by enlightenment. For the Gnostic; we need to know who we really are.

For the Gnostic; life was a goal of discovery of self. Where do your thoughts come from? For the Gnostic faith is secondary; it is only a stopgap until you have the knowledge-the direct experiential knowledge that is the essence of Gnosis.

For Gnostics, the quest for self-knowledge is identical with the quest to know God, because when we discover our deepest identity, we discover we are GOD. (Don't jump to conclusions.)

For the Gnostic believer knowledge in and of itself means nothing. Knowledge has different applications. Wisdom is using knowledge correctly in today's philosophy.

For the Gnostic the word Gnostic or Gnosis itself defined a way of living; a perception that was held. Gnosis is the knowledge that all is one. Gnosis is knowing nothing and loving everything. Witnessing life is not Gnosis. Living life is Gnosis and knowing that, "I am one with all."

The Gnostic yearns for experiential knowledge. The gospel is gnosis. The Gospel is that complete transformation is possible. The Gospel of Jesus is a blend of Mosheh (Moses)/ Messiah and the initiations of Osiris-Dionysus.

The Gnostics teach that when we realize gnosis, we will discover that our essential identity is the 'good.' In a moral sense, the greatest degree of good is the least degree of evil. This 'good' though; well; it is something else. The purpose of life is to consciously experience life and in doing so to feel good while doing it. Someone who through Gnosis has discovered their true self can live a spontaneous and natural life, motivated by the good within; for we are by nature good people. We won't need to 'become' good. Their life bears that "I have fought upon the earth for good, I have entered into the invisible, and I have finished my work. I have no stain. I have passed through the gates of darkness into light."

The greatest struggle between Christians and the secular world; is this idea that we are all good people. There are those who hold a staunch belief that we are born good and as we live we become stained by the world around us. Getting in touch with our true self, that part of us which carries compassion for others, respect, honor, loyalty, all these and many more aspects, is the journey of the goal to the Philosopher's Stone. There are those who believe that we need to get back in touch with this true inner self that we forget.

The other side of this coin comes from the Christians and the concept of original sin and being born in a state of sinful nature, we don't naturally turn to God/YHWH we need to be woken up and brought into the fold. It is our nature to sin, and we must struggle with this.

In time as Greek Culture blossomed in the Middle East, the Jewish people began to learn to read, write and speak Greek. Eventually the Septuagint was born. The Philosophers of Greek culture went to the Middle East. Their language went with them. The Jews learned to think like the Greeks and created many wonderful works.

Herein lays a truth that the Christians use to claim that the New Testament was originally written in Greek. The Septuagint was around for almost 400 years before Yahshua was born. There were many Jewish people who lived during that time who could speak Greek. However, a majority of scholars believe that these Greek speaking Jewish people did not live in Palestine but in Egypt.

The Greeks brought with them a different way of thinking and living. The root thoughts to find, "I am." (NOT YHWH), you. Can you find you? The root to find "I am," from whence do I come? Where do my thoughts originate. Why do I think? Why do

I dream? Where do my dreams come from? All of this was incorporated in the Septuagint. Then later on; it was seen in the Nag Hammadi library. A great many of the Apocryphal and Pseudepigraphal books also reflect this line of thinking.

Odysseus from Homer's *Odyssey* had to learn that he could not do it alone. How much of Christianity is the same? How much of Christianity is about the fact that we cannot make it through this life without YHWH? It was only when Odysseus realized that he was powerless that he was able to go home. It is only when we realize that we are powerless to affect the world around us and we turn on bended knee to Yahshua and YHWH that we become a "new" creature in Christ. It is a familiar story told over and over again, new names and new players but it is still the same story.

How many movies have this very same concept, the protagonist must turn to someone for help? Luke Skywalker could not blow up the Death Star without Han Solo. Peter Parker could not defeat the Green Goblin without Mary Jane Watson. Rose could not have survived the Titanic without Jack.

Laurie Stroud could not have defeated Michael Myers without doctor Loomis.

The Hellenization of the Middle East brought to the Jewish people a language that showed the complexity of human life. Before Judaism was changed by the Greek Empire, the Jewish people were trying to get life back to its most uncomplicated forms.

The Hebrew Language in and of itself shows you this. They don't have many words to express different ideas such as the English Language does. Like *love* in English, we love Cookies, and we love our family, we love our jobs. We use the same word in many contexts. We have destroyed our lives in the process.

For the Greeks; it was simpler but still more complex; there is love for GOD, or his type of love which is Agape; there is the love of family and friend which is philein; and still yet there is love that is sensual in nature which is Eros. We have taken erotic love and clipped it to pornography when it originally was not about sex; it was about the senses. Looking at beautiful artwork that was

76

moving of the soul and the spirit engaged emotion and the senses; therefore, the admiration of the painting or sculpture was Eros.

Because of this Hellenization; it is a given that the Gospels are symbolic: A leper is excommunicated, a resurrection is redemption, and the Bosom of Abraham is a place of spiritual execution; (purgatory is an insult to the sacrifice that Jesus made.)

The tomb is the body which is spiritually dead, finding the empty tomb represents the basic understanding we are not the body; it is also the cave of the cosmos.

Each of the names (and not just these, but all of them): Rachel, Rebecca, Sarah, Miriam (Mary) mean something special; just as do the names: Isaac, Jacob, Joseph, Abraham and Yahshua. An individual story defines a person. Words can have different definitions at different times. If we become fixated with words, we mistake the message for the meaning. The spoken word is an echo of thought, just as thought is an echo from someplace unknown.

77

This is the way that you look at the names: Joseph of Arimathea = 'Ram' or 'Rama - height , 'top' + 'theo' 'of God' = "highest of God." It may be that Joseph was a successor to the throne. In His family, David is the king, therefore Yahshua/ Jesus is king, we know that His brother James was the successor. Therefore, one way to see this is that Joseph of Arimathea is a brother of Jesus and James. At the least, he was a priest, may have been a High Priest, or even just as simple as a brother.

Let me give you another. Melchizedek. Gen. 14:8; It breaks into two words. Melchi and Zedek. Melchi comes from Malak; Zedek was originally Zadok. Malak is a messenger of Yahweh. Zadok is a just, righteous appointed one. Therefore, Melchizedek; the Just /Righteous Appointed Messenger of Yahweh went to visit Abraham.

The word translated "salvation" means preserved or made permanent; the word gentile refers to pagans who do not believe in YHWH. The root of culture is same as cult - colere - to worship.

Here's what we know:

1. The Septuagint was written in Greek. The Septuagint is from the 3rd Century BCE.

2. The language of the Nag Hammadi Library is Coptic and Greek; they are from the First and Second Century CE.

3. The Septuagint is 3-400 years older than the Nag Hammadi Library and the Dead Sea Scrolls.

4. The oldest Hebrew Text that we have is from 1000 CE (AD); this is the Massorctic text and it is in Leningrad Russia.

5. The Dead Sea Scrolls when compared with the Massoretic Text show that they are accurate.

But, the questions that were asked are the wrong ones; the questions need to be flipped. One such question is: Why doesn't the Massoretic text match the Septuagint? After all, the Septuagint is older than the Massoretic Text. Or, another one is; why can't we say that our Massoretic Text matches the DSS? The DSS are far older!!!

The Jews living in Alexandria that wrote in and spoke Greek wrote the Septuagint. It was written, according to legend, by 70 Hebrew/Greek scholars. These were HELLENIZED Israelites. They lived around the time that Alexander the Great conquered the known world. The Jews of Alexandria who knew the Tanak wrote the Septuagint to take their Scriptures to a new level of understanding. There is much to be said for the Greek thinking people, and the influence that they had over the Israelites.

Remember, it was Christians under the Bishop Theophilius that burned the Library of Alexandria.

The Bible or the Tanak was a book that was alive. There is a reason that the Talmud is as complex as it is. As we move through our lives, we change. Every day that we wake up we are someone new.

The Hasidic Jews and the Gnosties were trying to find a way to express their idea of the concept of a Creative Force. The Gnostics never denied that we learn as we live. We grow as we live.

There is no one that is doomed to be bound to a certain type of person. Humans have no fixed determinate nature. Existence precedes essence: we make ourselves up as we go along. Every day that we are alive has an impact on the next day. Everything that we experience that has touched our senses gets added to our personality and a character.

Character is determined by the element of emphasis that an individual's life is focused on, whether an idealist or a materialist.

As we live, we behave in accordance with what we perceive to be the facts, not the actual facts. We all are prone to jump to conclusions. We are inundated constantly with information. We think at lightning fast speeds. We are so busy being bombarded that we rarely take the time to slow it down. We make split second decisions continuously; it is just the way that we are. As a result, it seems that all too often that power, common opinion, and tradition are taken for truth.

Gnosis is not a theory to learn; it is a state of awakening. Gnosis is not an intellectual theory; it is a state of being. Gnostic faith is complete confidence in the process of life. Gnostic philosophy is extreme sports for the mind; its purpose is in knowing the now. Gnosticism is about finding that inner need to live and have a vital inner experience that we have somehow lost. Gnosticism is rooted firmly in the reality of this present moment. Lastly, Gnosticism is trusting that all of our situations are part of the curriculum of awakening.

There are many people, (and I am NOT pointing fingers at anyone, after all I used to be one), that believe that they have all of the knowledge that they need. I have found that there are many people who; think, or believe, that they have enough information and actually don't. Part of awakening is realizing and accepting that you have been asleep; that there is a wider world than previously envisioned.

There is a natural state of happiness that is our right; it's about living with joy. Happiness is a long-term state of mind that permeates the various faces of life and influences our outlook. Let me help you find what you deserve.

Paul writes to being in the world but not of it. I want to change the context that most Christians are familiar with. We must look at time. Being in the world and not of it, concerns itself with the fact that we live moment to moment. We are aware of time passing. There is a philosophy called Existentialism - as it applies to human beings - it is the difference between a thing as it is in itself.

The spiritualist understands that time is an illusion. There is no easy way to explain that there is nothing but the now.

I understand the NOW to be, an acknowledgement

that we can do nothing about the past. As we move from one second to the next second, we cannot effect the second that has passed. There is no guarantee for tomorrow. We cannot worry about something that we have no control over.

Influence maybe, control; never. The next second, is promised to no one. None of us know how long we have, so we have to live each day as it matters, that is the best that we can hope for.

The flesh that we inhabit is far too fragile. I fell in love with Brittany Murphy in her role in *Prophecy II: Ashtown* with Christopher Walken. There is a scene in which she and Christopher Walken are in a donut shop and she picks up the gun and shoots herself in the chest, and the look on her face is just priceless when she doesn't die. I don't know anyone who could have done it better. Then I saw her later in *Girl, Interrupted*. I was head-over-heels in love or smitten; and when she died, I was really hurt. She reminded me of just how truly fragile we are.

Death is the ultimate unfamiliar experience, the supreme opportunity to come to life.

All there is; is the NOW. You cannot jump one second into the future. Cannot make the future anything other than what will be. All of your actions, all of the actions of those around you create a future that is constantly in motion. But, because it is not promised, because you can't create it, it does not exist. The past is gone; never to be returned.

Stop reading. I mean it. don't read past this sentence, I want you to check your awareness, look at what you are experiencing, look at this moment for what it is.

Reaching back to an earlier statement that I made, about the origins of our thinking processes. I want you to think about this. Can you tell me why you are here? Can you explain to me the source of life? I am simply referring to our sentience, nothing more. We look in the mirror and see ourselves. We look at the world around us and marvel at life. We think, feel, believe, hurt, and live our lives knowing that we are going to die one day.

Does the beast of the field understand that it is going to die? Do the fish in the oceans, lakes and rivers know that they are going to die? Do the creatures that fly in the upper reaches of heaven know that one day it will fly no more?

Our consciousness cannot live more than minute to minute. We are aware, aware of what, I ask. There is nothing simpler than we are consciousness of experiences. Gnostics call the absolute mystery "consciousness, the one, the good, the beautiful and the true love; we are the absolute mystery." The Pagan Gnostic Lucian wrote "The best way to live is to be in the present moment and get along as best you can, trying to see the funny side of things." There is only the now, the past is gone, and the future is only a possibility. The present cannot be changed, but the future can be, you can't control it; but you can influence it. We do not exist in time; time exists in us. There is little that we have control of.

The concept; there is only the now can be misconstrued in a number of ways. It is not an excuse to completely let go of our responsibilities and care not for today or tomorrow. It is not a license to hedonism. We cannot deny history. The past is what it is. It is gone never to be retrieved, tomorrow is hope. The opening lines of the Constitution of the United States of America and the Declaration of Independence; that ALL MEN ARE CREATED EQUAL is a lie.

Humanity is a fragile creation. We are prone to all manner of illnesses, we are stricken with Diabetes, Leukemia, Cancer, AIDS, and there are too many to list. Our life span is from less than one day to as many as 10 decades. No one knows how many days you have.

There is only now, the universe is billions of years old. As scientists seek the middle of the universe; as they reach further and further into space looking for the light from the BIG BANG, they will tell us that it is X number of light years.

There is only the now. Can you grasp that for the creator of the Universe that this has been the blink of an eye? There is only the now; there is no word in Hebrew to describe the Western Concept of Eternity. For the Ancient Hebrew people, a covenant was from Everlasting to Everlasting; how long is that? Have you ever stopped to contemplate time? Have you ever actually tried to consider a thousand years? How about a million years? Do you have any idea what it means to live for even a hundred years? Time, it is an elusive and very fluid concept. No one really knows how long man has been here on this planet.

This idea of living in the now, it is a complex idea.

There is only now. Shift gears with me. It is important; all that you have control over; is each moment as it comes. You have no control over anything else. As each moment presents itself to you; you have a chance to make the best of it. When you are alone in your house and a stranger knocks on your door; and asks to use your phone. Can you give him all that you have? What attitude will you bring to the table?

This is the now; your attitude as each moment that you have been given comes to you. You may not be here the next moment.

I was told throughout my childhood that the truth will always come forward, no matter how hard one tries to hide it. Truth is infinite. Truth is not determined by human desire, or by human decree.

Truth knows no man; man knows no truth. Truth is the harmonization of the human mind and heart with what is. Truth is that mysterious, infinite, boundless reality; man a mere worm existing in minutes, hours and days and spending most of them foolishly. All philosophical ideas are relatively true; or false expressions of the absolute truth, which by its very nature is inexpressible. Absolute truth and ignorant humanity are divided by a vast interval of understanding.

I now firmly believe that the truth has finally come to us. I am inclined to believe that disguised in the teachings of the Bible is a book that was designed to pass on the mysteries. I think it is much more likely than not, that it is the truth. It makes a lot of sense to me.

All that man is or can ever hope to be depends upon his concept of God. We don't know what reality is. What do we know right now? What is it to be alive? What is this moment? What is living life this moment? Life is infinitely enigmatic. Life is a miracle. We've got to appreciate it. We are not living our lives; life is living through us. I am; I am aware. I have/am awareness. The 'I' is our being, it is what we are. It is the subject of experience; the "I." It is the sense of being. Identify with "awareness." It is who we are. Consciousness.

Yahweh is a whole lot bigger and a whole lot more incomprehensive than anything that any theologian of any religion has ever proposed. Yahweh is a big mind that contains the cosmos and is becoming conscious of itself through all conscious beings in the cosmos. The mystery of Yahweh's search to know itself is echoed in us. The inner sense of Yahweh is a quality of deeper psyche and not of reason. We are the mystery of Yahweh dreaming it is human. We are the universal being appearing to be human. Get to know who you truly are. Know yourself. Knowledge is central to Gnosticism, knowledge of who one really is.

This is us becoming YAHWEH. It is our awareness, the awareness of our self. YAHWEH knows himself. "I AM WHO I AM.", "I WILL BE WHAT I WILL BE." Can you identify the source of your thoughts or your identity? Expand your awareness.

We focus on what we experience instead of that

which we experience; when we focus that we are, not on what we are experiencing consciousness is both subjective and objective; we know the mystery through it manifestation as consciousness. We must ignore thoughts, feelings, sensations; and focus on the empty within which they rise and fall.

We must die to the insignificant smallness of our petty ego and resurrect to our deepest self - the self of all; the ultimate source of all is the absolute mystery. It is the gospel of absolute freedom. We need to let go of the idea that we are individuals with a "free-will." We are to give up attachment, but to realize our awareness. The awareness of our essential identity must increase, we must let go of the body.

We miss the point when we are lost in the wrong perspective. You are one with everyone and everything. When you know the mystery, the mystery knows itself. Our lives are the mystery wanting to love and be loved. In that moment, you will be completely sure that you exist now. We are not the limited thought, but the unknown thinker, we appear as the manifest, but we are the mystery.

What we experience is unique; our nature - the awareness - is the same. All of our senses exist with awareness. All we actually know is now. Awareness does not age & die, it exists outside of time. Awareness never changes, it is. Become a witness to experience, sensation, and thought. Everything else changes, awareness never does. As awareness, we are one. Awareness witnesses all of the moments of life. There are no yesterdays and no tomorrows. How does one isolate an experience? Experience is always embodied & therefore always suggestive.

Thoughts have no matter; they are not things that can be explained away. Our endless desires are a constant source of frustration. Desire rarely leads to satisfaction. Desire is a necessary part of our ego's need to be helped.

Consciousness is what we are, when our ego dies, we are resurrected as consciousness of God. Consciousness is unchanging. Consciousness is our being; eidolon is our image. When we realize that our true identity is the Son of God; it is time for our eidolon to die. We will no longer identify with the 'eidolon' and so will be literally selfless. The purpose of Gnostic initiation is to awaken in us recognition of our divine essence. We cannot die, as we were never born.

Archetype was first used by Philo. Archetypes appear to us in the form of symbolic images. Archetypes are the vocabulary of the psyche. The body has three distinct elements in its composition: Physis - the physical, also the shell, Psyche - the inner self, a deeper level of understanding that we are not our body, and nous - the intellect, Plotinus wrote, "the knowing principle." Sensations themselves are subjective events in the psyche. The Physis - the body is what we appear to be. Psyche is what we experience. Psychic initiation is primarily about personal growth, working on ourselves, "we are not a person, we are impersonal consciousness" it is the understanding of spiritual initiation.

We need to differentiate believing from knowing. We need to transform our negative personal characteristics into positive attributes. We do this by the secret knowledge that Yahshua delivered. We will begin to rouse ourselves from a collective coma that we mistake for life. We will spontaneously act well as a natural expression of our being. We will awaken from an unconscious stupor. Sometimes awakening takes years of personal transformation. There is no substitute for Gnosis either you are awake or you are not. Gnosticism is THE truth; it is, A truth; truth cannot be captured by concepts.

To realize Gnosis is to embrace the paradox. Pure philosophy is spiritual striving through constant contemplation to attain gnosis of God. It is the glorious rest of stillness without movement. "Experience must always be an experience of something, but detachment comes close to zero that nothing but GOD is rarefied enough to get into it, to enter the detached heart." We will know that all that happens is the will of God, which is the experience of unconditional acceptance and unshakeable faith. In Gnosticism, in the roots of mystery religions there were themes of hidden knowledge, mystical experiences, and death and rebirth. This knowledge can only come from revelation. The condition of the mind in which the Hermetic Philosopher wishes to operate is insight and higher reason.

Gnostics are consumed by their private quest for enlightenment, not by the goal of recruiting adherents. Gnosticism is better understood when approaching it from a Hermetic direction. Gnosticism and Hermeticism can be traced back to the same place, and the same time, Alexandria. Gnostic text is the authoritative teaching. Gnostics regarded the Canonized scripture as allegorical, the question begging to be asked and answered - was the writer a Gnostic - if so, why veil the message behind so dark a veil? If the writer was not a Gnostic, what benefit could be drawn for searching his text(s) allegorically?

Genuine religious experience is not only felt, it is acted out in a consistent pattern; human experiences are also meditated by the available symbols of a person's world. In the search for knowledge the highest wisdom is first to learn those things which have priority. As we grow and learn, we do so in stages, as they did in the Mystery Religions of old and can now be done in the Masonic Lodge, these stages became "stages of initiation." In the Christian world, the ritual of baptism is "an outward sign of inward change." It is ritual that is done in public so that other eyes can see the decision that you have made. The Catholic Church has a ritual that is called Confirmation that represents the growth of the believer, and the believer takes on a new name.

The Jesuits restored Gnosticism in the Council of Trent in 1493; they saw the truth; but it was too late.

In most cultures and ways of life that practice some form of initiation; they are all different each in their own uniqueness, but there are usually just 3 stages of rebirth; The first stage of initiation is purification and struggle. The next stage of initiation is death of old self. The last stage is the reward. The trials of life are the purification. The death of the old self is that final moment of, "I have had it." The last stage is the new person that you have become. You are now GOLD.

To learn to think intelligently requires more time and effort than any other profession known to man, and is only to be realized through the most exacting disciplines. Understanding is the rarest of all faculties. Understanding is the ultimate stage of knowledge; it is the perfect realization of the purpose and meaning of things. The power to become God is in rising above the masses full of the right knowledge.

The home of the Hermetic Gnostic is in the projected mind of God. Only right belief brings salvation, therefore wrong belief brings damnation. What do you believe your creator to be? Remember that most of the things we claim we know are actually just opinions that we believe. We have heard them from others and claim them as our own. You must find your own way to the creator of your essence.

Today, just as the Church has rituals that mark all kinds of events in the personal life, the Messiah and his followers practiced rituals as well, one of them was the raising of Lazarus; this was an initiation; pure and simple. "The secret ritual Jesus/Yahshua betrayed was the resurrection" of Osiris & Horus - *"The Living Resurrection Ceremony."* In the Greek anastasis - resurrection and awakening - the resurrection is awakening the Christ within. *The Gospel of Thomas* may be older than the canon gospels. It is not meant to convey information, but to awaken. The *Levitikon*, which is a *Gospel of*

97

John, describes Yahshua as an initiate of the Mysteries of Osiris. The Montgomery document says that Miriam of Bethany was a priestess of a cult.

Galilee was known as the land of the Gentiles, and was more diverse in culture than Samaria, Galilee had no capital, no hierarchy of priests, no temple, and had influences on various religions & wealthy; it was not as rustic as it is portrayed. In the *Gospel of John* there is no nativity, no description of birth, the first 11-18 verses of chapter 1 is in fact almost Gnostic; as a whole, the text is more mystical. For *Matthew, Mark, Luke* they all focus on Galilee. The wedding at Cana shows he moved in social circles. In *John* they are in Jerusalem & a wedding at Cana, there is Nicodemus, Joseph, and Lazarus. Though the gospels do not agree with place of birth, they do agree that he began in Galilee. There is even a Rite of Misraim/ Mithras. Messiah is one that is smeared with Holy Oil. Miriam is Sophia. The Messiah/Christ is the anointed one, and the person who anointed him was a woman Mk 14:9. It is obvious that Mary the Magdalene & Mary of Bethany could be the same.

Raymond K. Hedgespeth

As it is understood today, the salvation that
Yahshua offered came unlooked for and
unexpected; it was unknown to all ancient
philosophy, and unlike anything found in ancient
religion. Messiah's most prominent activity is
teaching. However, He is never called teacher by
His disciples or the faithful; they call him Lord. The
label 'teacher' is used by the outsiders, the scribes,
the Pharisees, the tax collectors, the Herodians, and
the Sadducees. In *Mark*, everyone calls Him
Teacher but the afflicted. Messiah does not argue
with the Scribes and Pharisees about the nature of
YHWH, or even himself, even with His closest
friends; He never gives a clear answer.

It is evident that the last supper was a pagan rite.
The Jews would never drink blood. It was
considered an abomination. He was delivered to
Pilate as a doer of evil, equivalent to a sorcerer.

It is pretty much accepted that no soldier would
gamble for worthless rags. Heaven & Hell are not
places to go when we die; they are occupied by
those who are asleep and those who awake. Paul
does not describe his experience in physical or

psychological terms, but with religious symbols. The "earliest" known Gnostic teacher is found in the 8th chapter of Acts – Simon Magus.

I read a work some time ago that said Gnosticism should not return; I would have to say that I am in serious disagreement. The time for Gnosticism to return to the forefront of the mind is here. Christianity is dying and it will be dead and ready for burial when the Gnostics and the Kabbalists stand up and start shouting from the rooftops what happened in our history and how the Christians have not stood up to the image that they have portrayed and that they have truly been an evil, and an evil that needs to be stamped out.

I think the time has passed, and it passed a very long time ago, that someone should take all of the notes that are available on Kabbalah, Gnosticism, and Hermeticism, and even the Mysteries themselves, and put them in a Bible that is geared for the Gnostic. I think the time has long since passed for a promising study Bible for the Gnostics. I don't have the resources that I need or I would undertake the project myself.

I see a serious study Bible in my mind's eye with copious footnotes, cross references, and a concordance, dictionary and the Gnostic texts, all in one source. I have said before, I was a Christian for a great many years, and I have owned a number of Bibles, some of them simple, with no extra material, while quite a few have been very serious study Bibles. I see a Bible for Gnostics in my mind's eye taking the best that these have to offer and imitating the style and putting the Gnostic twist on it, in the notes and in the translation.

We need a Bible that differentiates between the different names that were used to denote which "God" was doing the talking, whether it was El, Elohim, YHWH, Adonai, El-Shaddai, or whomever. We need a Bible that will give footnotes and cross-references to other verses that are mystical in the same nature and will give further support to the belief just as the Christian Bibles do. It can be done; it needs to be done. There needs to be a rally of support from the world over.

I know myself I would love to have one and I would pay whatever the price for one, as long as it was truthful and unbiased. I think the time has come for the Gnostics to have a Bible of their own. I know I am tired of having to use a Christian Bible to study the Gnostic religion out of. I put so many notes in the margins that eventually I have to buy another Bible and spend 3-4 days changing my notes from one to another, and then I go through another 6 months to a year and then the process starts all over again, as I learn and add to my knowledge. I would think that many Gnostics would agree that the time for us to have our own Bible has come and is upon us.

Those of us who want to follow the Gnostic, Hermetic, way need to make a strong showing in numbers as Christians did. We need not use guns and resort to murder as the Christians of Rome did; but we need to band together and come together as ONE. We need to start buying these books and leaving them around for people to see, hopefully they will pick them up and start to read them. We need to combat TBN. We need to show the world the truth, and yes, the truth hurts, but nevertheless the truth needs to be told.

Raymond K. Hedgespeth

Hermes Trismegistus, provided the wisdom of the light, greatest of the philosophers, greatest of the kings, greatest of the priests. "The goal of gnosis is to become God." But, it must not be taken out of context.

Given that most of our action is economically or socially motivated, we need to learn to shut out the mundane. If we cannot control our thoughts, we cannot control our intentions, and then we cannot control our actions.

As I close out this book, there are a few thoughts that I want you to take with you. The first is this; in the entire history of our species; there hasn't been one person who has even come close to suggesting that he or she knows where our thoughts come from.

Look at yourself; I mean really look at yourself, see the marvelous machine that you are. It is time to stop living this life as if you are worthless and without promise. I posit this; either every human on this planet is worth something or none of us are.

I have studied the human race for a long time. We

are very judgmental. We put each other under tremendous amounts of pressure. We criticize so much; and do so without regard to why we are doing it. I won't name them all, but we judge and criticize our weight, the size of her breasts, the color of our hair, the color of our skin, the things we like to do or don't like, we judge sports players, we laugh and scorn and ridicule those who are different from us; we push so many people away for so many reasons. When there is one aspect of our lives that draws us together more than any other.

WE ALL WANT UNCONDITIONAL ACCEPTANCE. We all want to be loved for who we are, what we are, in spite of our faults. We want to be wanted by another; we want to feel as if we belong. We want to feel needed, important, and as if we matter. We want our opinions to matter.

We put each other under so much stress; we are so quick to judge. I have a question. What does it really matter if someone is heterosexual, homosexual, transgender or whatever? Who really cares and why should you care?

The Bible and Christianity have a large following

for one simple reason: there is someone who will accept you regardless of what it is that you have done. There is that element of unconditional acceptance that draws so many people from all walks of life.

The Philosopher's Stone; allow the life that you are living to have an impact on you. You need to see yourself for whom and what you truly are. Understand without doubting; that you matter, and that because you matter everyone else does too. Everyone on this planet is designed the same way. Every human regardless of skin color, national origin, ethnic background, language of choice, religious or philosophical leanings, sexual orientation, height, weight, social class, or gender; we are all the same. Every one of us matters. We are all special; and it is time to live as if we are. We need to look out for one another. We need to be giving of the best that we have to give to each and every single one of us.

Give of your time, yourself, your money, everything that doesn't belong to you anyway. We are only here for a little while and everything that we have is simply loaned to us any way.

That which is inside you that has no physical substance; that is who and where you really are. Find yourself and tell me all about it; I am waiting to hear from you.

Raymond Hedgespeth

POBox 800

Mauston, WI 53948

CONCLUSION

Is the Bible a book that is Allegorical, Mythical, Metaphysical, and/or Gnostic, based on the Mystery traditions, or is it a straight forward historical book that has a few mistakes because the hand of man is not perfect? The decision of course is yours and yours alone to make. How you interpret all the material I have given you, and what would you do with it, that is totally up to you. I do think that in my humble opinion that the Golden Dawn and the rest of the material that is based on the Bible and the archaic and ruthless dealings of the Catholic Church need to be reexamined and gone over with a new light based on the information I have given here.

Remember, after having read this, going back to the beginning of this little book, this isn't necessarily about religion. I have used the Bible, because, as I said earlier, it is a book with which I am intimately familiar and it served my needs for expressing my thoughts and the material that I have learned.

You don't really need the Bible to lead a good life,

there are millions of people who are good, decent and caring people who don't read the Bible, don't attend Church, or are religious in any sense of the word.

The message is truly simple.

The PHILOSOPHER'S STONE is your heart.

ABOUT THE AUTHOR

Raymond is a historian of the Middle East and how the Bible came to us. As he has grown in his studies over the years, he has been down many roads and carved many paths. He has had to cut his way through a jungle of opinions and has been starved for knowledge. This is but the first book that Raymond has written; he has several more that are in production to share with you.

Raymond encourages you to write to him with feedback and criticism. He does have plans for a revision of this book in the years to come. The reason for this, is that Raymond has read many books by several author's that have not been updated as knowledge has increased; thereby creating problems in the dedicated study that Raymond has undergone.

It is only fair to you that Raymond share with you as he learns more and is able to absorb what he learns and give it to you in his own words. Raymond believes in being true and honest and sharing that which he knows to be the truth as he understands it. To do otherwise would be to lie, that is against his integrity.